A Mindful Diet
Four Weeks to Eating Awareness

A Mindful Diet

FOUR WEEKS TO EATING AWARENESS

Jeanie Seward-Magee

Order this book online at www.trafford.com
or email orders@trafford.com

Most Trafford titles are also available at major online book retailers.

Note for Librarians: A cataloguing record for this book is available from Library
and Archives Canada at www.collectionscanada.ca/amicus/index-e.html

Printed in Victoria, BC, Canada.

ISBN: 978-1-4269-1439-3

*Our mission is to efficiently provide the world's finest, most comprehensive
book publishing service, enabling every author to experience success.
To find out how to publish your book, your way, and have it available
worldwide, visit us online at www.trafford.com*

Trafford rev. 8/21/2009

 www.trafford.com

North America & international
toll-free: 1 888 232 4444 (USA & Canada)
phone: 250 383 6864 ♦ fax: 812 355 4082

Also by

Jeanie Seward-Magee

A Mindful Way – Eight Weeks to Happiness

(2005)

www.amindfulway.com

This book is dedicated to the memory of my dear parents
Megan and Dick Seward

And to the memory of my two young nephews
Maarten and Thomas Seward
"Together in Eternity"

Foreword

"What shall I eat today?" is a very deep question. You will find that as you practice awareness of consumption and looking deeply at what you eat, your habit energy may soon begin to change. And with mindful eating you may cultivate the seeds of compassion and understanding that could strengthen your will to do something to help hungry and lonely people to be nourished in many other ways.

Keeping your body healthy is a wonderful way of expressing gratitude. If you are healthy, then everyone will benefit from this. We are what we consume. If you look deeply into how much and what items you consume everyday, you will get to know your own nature very well.

The simple practices outlined in this new book by Jeanie Seward-Magee, "A Mindful Diet – Four Weeks to Eating Awareness" are a wonderful introduction to the art of practicing mindful eating for life.

Thich Nhat Hanh

A Mindful Diet

FOUR WEEKS TO EATING AWARENESS

Diets don't work, because you haven't changed your eating habit energy.
Mindful eating does work, because it changes your
eating habit energy, not what you are eating!

Contents

Introduction to "A Mindful Diet"

Recently, I got myself a wonderful personal trainer. His name is Winston Edward Seward-Magee. He is a small mixed-breed ball of fluff – a tiny Maltese/Shih Tzu puppy. I had never felt I needed a personal trainer; however, Winston Edward has been the best teacher of mindfulness, mindful eating, and mindful exercise that I could have ever found. The reason he is such a great personal mindfulness trainer is that when he walks, he walks; when he eats, he eats; when he sleeps, he sleeps; when he barks, he barks; and when he sees a new doggie or human friend he is totally there for them – aware of only them. That is essentially what mindfulness is all about: moment-by-moment total awareness.

So, keeping in mind the well-used acronym, KISS - "keep it simple, sweetheart", let's go together on this mindful journey of changing your eating habits for four weeks, then maybe for life, with A Mindful Diet – Four Weeks to Eating Awareness.

In this age of busy-ness, this book can be used in a number of different ways, and of course which way you choose is entirely your choice. So select any of the behaviours, exercises, or ideas from this book that suit you and your lifestyle, and apply them regularly.

"Tell me and I'll forget. Show me, and I may not remember. Involve me, and I'll understand."
-NATIVE AMERICAN PROVERB

Once you have chosen the behaviour that is most like you, and have chosen the Mindful Diet Eating Exercises that you wish to follow, please remember that it is only with practice, practice and more practice, that any of the ideas given in this book will give you lifetime changes in your eating habits. As a person eats, so you are.

Please be aware that any habit will take at least four weeks to change. This is because your habit energies are extremely strong. Just as you first have to walk around the block before you can even consider running a marathon, so old habit energies have to be replaced at each meal or with each mouthful with the new habit energy of mindfulness, concentration, and insight, before you can become fully engaged in a lifetime of mindful eating.

Also maybe write a journal to assist you with your insights and feelings, your defeats and victories. Just as you might write a travel journal, this is your own A Mindful Diet journey/journal for at least the next four weeks. Writing, it is said, helps reduce stress, assists in lifting depression, and boosts your immune systems. Writing is a wonderful way to keep track of and learn to change your eating habits for life.

"Intentions and results are always the same. Intentions practiced give results."

-JIM QUINN

What is Mindful Eating?

Dr. Susan Albers, Ph. D., tells us in her wonderful book, "Eating Mindfully"

"Mindfulness, and more specifically, the notion of a mindful diet, is not a new idea. It is a centuries-old practice based on the ancient common-sense Eastern wisdom of mindfulness or "pure awareness".

You can apply mindfulness to any part of your life at any time; however, when you start eating mindfully, you may find you become aware, conscious, and mindful of many other aspects of your life. This includes mindfulness of your mind, body, thoughts, and feelings.

It is about becoming conscious of how, why, when, where, and what you are eating. It is about being aware of your emotions – your feelings around food – and it is about enjoying eating, and eating what you enjoy, rather than following a diet.

There are no menus or recipes to follow. Instead, there are just a few simple, mindful ideas that you can practice whenever you are eating. When you are closely in touch with what is going on inside of yourself, you will be aware of what is happening outside yourself; that is, what is actually on your plate or in your mouth about to be swallowed.

Understanding the why, what, when, where, and how of your eating patterns and habits allows you to become more comfortable, more compassionate, and in the final analysis less judgmental with yourself."

"There are no perfect beings, and there never will be."

-HENRY MILLER

How to Use "A Mindful Diet"

This book is called A Mindful Diet. Did you know the word *diet* comes from the Latin word *diaeta* and the Greek word *diaita*, both meaning "a way of life"? This book, then, is not a diet book; rather, it is about mindful eating and making small habit changes. Ultimately, it is about choosing a new way of life in which you decide what changes you wish to make. This book is about your personal choices.

A Mindful Diet is a book about knowing what you are eating and really enjoying your food. It is about making small daily changes for a minimum of four weeks, so that over time you will have the tools – the new habit energies – to make lifetime changes.

Eating mindfully is about making small eating habit changes such as thinking twenty percent less, changing portion sizes, or eating one hundred calories a day more or fewer, which means you'll gain or lose ten pounds in one year. Small changes do make a big difference. Just remember that the bigger the habit change, the higher the fall-off rate, the smaller the habit change, the higher the success rate. This book is both easy and inexpensive to follow, and it offers flexible individual ideas. Make use of whatever you find easiest for you; it can be combined with other regimens and can assist you in changing a lifetime of eating habits.

What type of eater are you? There is way to categorize eating types. Are you a **meal stuffer**, stuffing yourself with large portions or taking second helpings, or are you a **snack grazer**, grazing on snacks all day? Perhaps you're a **party binger**, using food as a backdrop to socializing, or a **restaurant indulger**, living on an expense account? Perhaps you are a **desktop diner**, eating while doing something else at your desk or table? These five eating types come from a wonderful book called "Mindless Eating" by Brian Wansink Ph.D. Mindless eating is what we all tend to do, which is the complete opposite of mindful eating! Mindful eating is what A Mindful Diet is about.

I suggest you carry this book with you at all times. It has been printed in a small size so it will fit into your purse or pocket, so you can refer to it and reinforce the ideas in it whenever you eat, shop for food, or even think about eating or shopping for food! If there is a goal at all, it is to learn the practice of mindfulness itself, not trying to lose weight or gain a new body. It is practicing being truly present where you are with your eating habits and cultivating your ability to be totally aware of the present moment – the "now" – in your body, thoughts, feelings, and actions.

This book is different from other books because it is designed to help people to eat in awareness. Diets don't work because people lose weight only to gain it back again. Mindful eating, based on the centuries old Buddhist practice of mindfulness, will work, because it changes your eating habit energy, not what you are eating

This book is not about depriving yourself (traditional dieting), because your body and mind will fight this, as will your daily environment. I recommend trying to make just three small changes every day for four weeks and continue these for the rest of your life.

"In the long run, we shape our lives, and we shape ourselves. The process never ends until we die. And the choices we make are ultimately our own responsibility."
-ELEANOR ROOSEVELT

We all have choices, so you could use a different idea/exercise with every meal or one for each day. On the other hand, perhaps you will use just one single idea for the next four weeks, or perhaps a single idea for the rest of your life! Or follow my "A Mindful Diet" Contract. Whichever path you choose, in four weeks you will begin to see a change in your eating habits, and the beginning of lifetime changes.

Mindfulness of Body, Mind and Feelings

Mindfulness of Body: Awareness of your body's messages is a great starting place. Become aware of the specific signs your body is giving you of hunger and thirst. We are all unique so watch your own body for the signs it gives you, for each of us they will be different. Is your body telling you it is really hungry, or is it not really hungry? Is it telling you are full and are you paying attention to it when it says to stop eating? You can either choose to listen to your body or choose to ignore it. Your body knows when it is still hungry and full; learn to listen and to respond. Stressful emotional eating and physical hunger are very different; learn to recognize the difference. When you are eating how aware or mindful are you of what you are eating? Do you really taste the food you have in your mouth? Different foods have such a variety of textures, sounds and even smell; observe these closely and recognize which ones you like the most when you are eating.

Mindfulness of Mind: How aware are you of the thoughts in your mind in this very moment? Begin to take notice of them. Begin to identify the "I should" and the "I should not" thoughts and then see how they can determine different behavours. Always remember that thoughts are impermanent and also do not have to be followed. When you are eating do you snack or binge; are you really aware of each wonderful mouthful of food?

Mindfulness of Feelings: Feeling or emotions are so important to get in touch with and to learn what they are really about, however again realize they too are impermanent and will pass. Some feelings may want to make you eat and some not want to eat. Boredom, stress, grief, sadness or happiness can make you think you need to eat or not need to eat. Begin to notice feelings that start you eating, or may stop you from eating. Knowing how to handle your feelings and leaning how to cope with them in constructive ways can change your eating habit energies. Name the feeling and know what it is really about.

In his book, "Mindless Eating", Dr. Wansink writes about recognizing emotional hunger. He says, "It develops suddenly rather than gradually. It appears above the neck, perhaps just thinking about the taste of a certain foods, rather than below the neck feeling the actual hunger in your stomach. Emotional hunger is usually unrelated to time (such as well before a mealtime) and it often persists after a meal and despite being full. Emotional eating can lead to guilt and shame."

"To be always intending to live a new life, but never find time to set about it —this is as if a man should put off eating and drinking from one day to another till he be starved and destroyed."

-Sir Walter Scott

Greater Awareness of Eating

Mindful eating includes being aware of all your senses. By using your eyes, ears, nose, tongue, and fingers, you become fully aware of how your food looks, sounds, smells, tastes, and feels.

For example, by picking up a potato chip or a raspberry or a raisin, by looking at its colour, its shape, and its size, and by tasting the saltiness or sweetness on your fingers as you pick it up, and by noting the taste of it when you put it on your tongue, you are using all of your senses.

Next, you are aware of the loud crunch or squish of each bite, and the noise the chewing makes in your head. As you eat this food, you take note of the rough or smooth texture against your tongue and the pressure of your teeth grinding together.

When you are watchful and aware, you notice how your stomach expands and feels fuller. You experience each bite from start to finish by slowing down every aspect of the eating process. You become fully aware of each movement as you swallow. You are fully aware of the food's aroma. You begin to notice the sweetness, sourness, saltiness, bitterness, astringent or pungent tastes in your food. Finally, you are fully in touch with the psychological feeling of satisfaction you derive from eating.

Now you are beginning to eat with awareness, or mindfully! What a wonderful eating meditation!

"If we could see the miracle of a single flower clearly, our whole life would change."

-THE BUDDHA

Attitude, Gratitude, and Acceptance

"I accept that my eating concerns are creating much emotional distress and suffering in my life. I am grateful for this deep awareness."

"I choose to accept my body and weight just as they are in this moment. I am so grateful for this knowledge and acceptance."

"Committing to accept myself as I am just now is a choice only I can make. I am grateful for my awareness and this deeper insight."

"I accept that my genetic inheritance strongly influences my body shape and weight. I am grateful for my wonderful parents and grandparents and their genetic legacy."

"I accept how important it is for me to eat mindfully in order to live a healthy life. I am very grateful for my present health."

"Acceptance only comes from within me. I don't seek it from the outside. I am grateful for my changed attitude."

"I accept that my worth is not reflected by my weight and shape; rather, my worth is determined by who I am as a whole person. I am grateful that I am unique."

These attitudes, gratitudes and acceptances come from many different sources and for this I am truly grateful. Unfortunately, at the time I recorded them I was forgetful (one of our greatest enemies!) and did not take note of where I obtained them, however I am truly grateful to all the unnamed authors for their mindful and insightful words. Thank you all so very much.

"A man does not learn to understand anything unless he loves it."

-JOHANN WOLFGANG VON GOETHE

The Five Contemplations

The Five Contemplations are said before every meal in many mindfulness practice communities and centers throughout the world. They are the equivalent of saying grace or blessing foods that are about to be eaten, and they are a wonderful form of gratitude for being thankful for the food on your table and on your plate.

The Five Contemplations written, and then updated in October 2007, by Thich Nhat Hanh are later considered individually, one at a time. The idea is to apply some practical ideas for working with them to enable you to become aware of your eating habits over the next four weeks.

THE FIVE CONTEMPLATIONS

*This food is a gift of the Earth, the sky, numerous
living beings, and much hard work.*

*May I eat with mindfulness and gratitude,
so as to be worthy to receive this food.*

*May I recognize and transform my unwholesome
mental formations, especially my greed,
and learn to eat with moderation.*

*May I keep my compassion alive by eating in such a
way that I reduce the suffering of living beings, preserve
our planet, and reverse the process of global warming.*

*I accept this food so that I may nurture my sisterhood
and brotherhood, strengthen my community,
and nourish my ideal of serving all beings.*

THE FIRST CONTEMPLATION

"This food is a gift of the Earth, the sky, numerous living beings, and much hard work."

- When preparing your food, do a vegetable chopping meditation by focusing on your breathing while cutting up vegetables for your meal. Say to yourself:

- Say before eating, "In this food I see the entire universe supporting my existence."

- Take time to relax before eating. Say grace or a prayer of thanks for the food in front of you, or just close your eyes for a few moments, contemplating the food you will put on your plate. Say to yourself:

  "My plate is now empty.
  However, I know that it will soon
  be filled with precious food."

- When you put the food on your plate, take stock of where the food has come from. Say to yourself:

  "My plate is filled with food.
  I am aware that each morsel is
  the result of much love
  And the hard work of those
  who have produced it."

THE SECOND CONTEMPLATION

*"May I eat with mindfulness and gratitude,
so as to be worthy to receive this food."*

- Use this little mantra while eating:

  With your first mouthful, say to yourself:
  "I promise to practice kindness."
  With your second mouthful, say to yourself:
  "I promise to assist in relieving
  the suffering of others."
  With your third mouthful, say to yourself:
  "I promise to see others' joy as my own."
  With the fourth mouthful, say to yourself:
  "I promise to learn the way of
  nonattachment and equanimity."

- Don't eat and work at the same time. Try never to multi-task, especially while eating. Don't eat while sitting in front of your TV, computer, or at your desk. Don't eat while listening to the radio or when reading a book, newspaper, or magazine. When you eat – just eat. This is the key to preventing mindless eating habits.

- Don't skip meals. This allows your battery to get low and results in you overloading your circuits by later stuffing yourself or pigging out.

- Don't rush your eating. Try to chew each mouthful at least ten times: twenty or thirty is better! Put your fork down between every bite. Make small changes, bite by bite.

- Choose a peaceful, distraction-free location for your meals. In addition to finding a special place for eating, also find a special space and time to tune into your body's feelings.

- Become a member of the "Clean Plate Club," taking only enough food on a small plate and eating very slowly. Portion size makes a huge difference. This way you never have to count calories, because you are mindful of the look, smell, colours, and taste of your food. You are also mindful of where you are eating and who has brought this food to you.

THE THIRD CONTEMPLATION

"May I recognize and transform my unwholesome mental formations, especially my greed, and learn to eat with moderation."

- Ask yourself, "Am I truly hungry?" Focus internally and don't ignore hunger pangs; you will simply get hungrier and more likely to overindulge. Allow yourself to eat whenever you feel hungry. Don't ignore hunger and your body's natural cues (stomach rumbling, low energy).

- Ask yourself: "Am I eating for emotional reassurance or stress relief?"

- Be fully in the moment while you are eating. Make sure your attention is fully focused on your food. Be alert and observant of your thoughts; when your mind wanders, keep bringing your attention back to your food.

- "Forgotten eating" is when you pick at food, and become un-mindful. This leads you to believe that you have little or no control.

- Ask yourself: "Am I full?" and then simply **stop**. Just like a "full stop" in English, or a "period" in North America, stop or take a time-out – a period of rest. Don't continue to eat – to stuff yourself – when you are full. Be aware of when your hunger is satisfied. Eat slowly; contemplating each bite, because it takes approximately twenty minutes for your body to tell you it is satiated.

THE FOURTH CONTEMPLATION

*"May I keep my compassion alive by eating
in such a way that I reduce the suffering
of living beings, preserve our planet, and
reverse the process of global warming."*

- Practice seasonal hundred-mile food consumption, thus reducing your carbon footprint. This means eating only food that is grown or raised within one hundred miles of where you live.

- Enjoy what you eat, and eat what you enjoy. "Live to eat" rather than "Eat to live."

- Make a conscious effort to eat what your body really likes and to enjoy it – in moderation. Food is just what it is, and should never be categorized as "good" or "bad."

- Become consciously aware of and pay attention to your food choices for your body type and its nutritional needs. Eat more vegetables, and try to make at least half of your meals completely vegetarian.

The Fifth Contemplation

"I accept this food so that I may nurture my sisterhood and brotherhood, strengthen my community, and nourish my ideal of serving all beings."

- Be non-judgmental, accepting, and compassionate first toward yourself and then others. Let go of critical thoughts and emotions without reacting.

- Join a faith centre. The people you meet there can become your family or friends, or the centre can be a place of worship for you.

"Understanding is my only career in life"

-THICH NHAT HANH

- Be aware that mindful eating is an ongoing journey, and it starts with a single bite. You can begin anew with the very next bite!

- Be kind to yourself and all whom you meet. Find ways to serve others daily. Never be concerned about action, only inaction.

- Be diligently watchful of pre- and post-eating feelings. Mindfulness means noticing, rather than evaluating; it is a whole new way of being.

- Be aware of your needs, so that you actually meet them. Be aware of others' needs and try to assist them in fulfilling their needs.

- Treat yourself to a retreat. It is a wonderful way to reflect, renew, laugh, share, be still, and a marvelous way to celebrate your life.

My "A Mindful Diet" Contract

"Life can be
found only
in the present
moment. The
past is gone, the
future is not yet
here, and if we
do not go back to
ourselves in the
present moment,
we cannot be in
touch with life."

-THICH NHAT
HANH

Choose two mindful eating exercises from the "Eating Action Exercises" Section of this book (just two pages ahead) that personally appeal to you. Choose the two you feel you can practice simply and easily for the next four weeks. Write them in below, and also fill them in on your "Beginning Anew - My Habit Energy Change Chart" on the next page.

Date and Sign them. When you sign something you are making a commitment to yourself. Who better to commit to than yourself?

1. Before each meal I shall recite (or think about) "The Five Contemplations".

2. ....
....

3. ....
....

Day and Date:.............................
Signed:.......................................

Beginning Anew

How to use My Habit Energy Change Chart

Your First Habit Energy Change has already been filled into your Chart for you; it is "The Five Contemplations"! This will become, with each meal, your First Habit Energy Change for the next four weeks. Say it to yourself silently, or better still out loud, before you begin eating every meal. Try it for a few days; then if you decide you prefer to say another gratitude or a formal Grace that is completely your choice. However Thich Nhat Hanh has written these words with the greatest of care and deepest understanding.

Now fill in your Second and Third Habit Energy Change on both My "A Mindful Diet" Contract and My Habit Energy Change Chart. Choose these from the Eating Action Exercises or Mindful Eating Ideas sections of this book. Choose carefully two exercises or ideas that you feel you would most benefit from and are maybe a wee bit of a stretch for you!

Now for the next four weeks you will use these Three Habit Energy Changes every time you eat to begin to alter your eating style. Remember change always starts with very small steps; this is always the better way! Also, don't forget to fill in your start date at the top of the Chart and your actual days of the week in the fifth column before you begin.

Now this is very important. At the end of each day on the Chart write "Yes" or "No" in the appropriate area of the Chart, if you did or did not follow any of your three Habit Energy Changes before eating each meal. You can maybe even write in a Personal Journal some comments about your progress each day. Be completely honest with yourself. Always celebrate your victories, however, please do not beat yourself up if you forgot or did not make a Habit Energy Change at one of your daily meals.

Right now, or with the next meal, you can always begin anew. Make good use of the ideas in the Supportive Practices section to assist you, or reread and put into practice any part of this book that is helpful to you. And please remember any habit energy usually takes a minimum of four weeks to change! Good luck and practice well!

My Habit Energy Change Chart

First Habit Energy Change The Five Contemplations	Second Habit Energy Change	Third Habit Energy Change	Day Number Four Weeks to Eating Awareness	Start Date And Days of the Four Weeks
			1	
			2	
			3	
			4	
			5	
			6	
			7	
			8	
			9	
			10	
			11	
			12	
			13	
			14	
			15	
			16	
			17	
			18	
			19	
			20	
			21	
			22	
			23	
			24	
			25	
			26	
			27	
			28	
Congratulations!	Wow, I have completed four weeks!	Now I shall eat mindfully forever!		

Eating Action Exercises

Today, while I eat a meal, I do nothing else. I do not talk; I do not read a newspaper, a magazine, or a book; I do not listen to music or the radio; and I do not watch television or drive a vehicle while eating.

Today, I eat a larger lunch and a smaller dinner.

Today, I eat only three meals.

Today, I eat six small meals.

Today, I do not to skip any meals.

Today, I use small plates, bowls, and cups to consume all my food and drinks. It is called portion control.

Today, I use one small bowl for all my meals. I only fill it up once for each meal.

Today, I make it inconvenient to get snacks. I put them somewhere that forces me to make a great effort to find them. Or I simply don't keep them anywhere at home or at work.

Today, I buy only the food I need for today. I avoid big warehouse stores because the more food I have at home, the less mindfully I will consume it.

Today during each meal I chew each mouthful of food at least ten times.

Today, I have one silent meal.

Today, I pause after five minutes when eating every meal.

Today, I take twenty minutes to eat one plate of food.

Today, I take a raisin or a fresh berry and place it on my tongue. I close my eyes and take at least five minutes to eat it. It is a marvelous eating meditation.

Today, I start last and finish last when dining with friends.

Today, if dining out, I choose only two out of the following three: a drink, an appetizer, or a dessert.

Today *no* food is off limits. I know that if I deny myself something I will tend to crave it more. If I eat something I crave, I only eat half my usual amount.

Today, I eat a meal consisting of one-half portion of vegetables and one-half of a salad.

Today, at dinner I serve only vegetables family-style on the table, and I leave the proteins in the kitchen.

Today, I change my "table environment", either by moving my place of eating or by setting up my table differently. It helps me to make changes in my mind.

Today, I serve myself 20 percent less than I think I will eat, or add 20 percent more fruit and vegetables to my plate.

Today, I buy smaller packages when shopping – I will then serve myself less.

Today, I use only tall, skinny drink glasses. I am an illusionist.

Today, I use my side plates rather than my dinner plates to serve up my food.

Today, I will eat all my meals with chopsticks.

Today, I leave a little food on my plate at the end of each meal.

Today, I treat myself to breakfast in bed.

Today, I take one ten-minute walk. Fifteen or twenty minutes are better!

Today, I invite a friend to join me on my walks – an exercise buddy.

Today, I only order an appetizer-sized portion of food when eating at a restaurant.

Today, when I break-my-fast, I eat a healthy breakfast.

Today, I deprive myself of nothing – just cut everything in half, and only eat half of that.

Today, I begin a journal of my daily eating and exercise.

Today, I make an appointment with myself (and write it in my calendar) to go for a walk or take an exercise class.

Today, I treat myself to a lovely scarf or tie, or a small bunch of flowers; there are other things besides chocolates and ice cream for treats.

Today, I eat five vegetables and four fruits. It is one of the keys to a healthy body.

Today, when eating out, I share a course with someone else.

Today, when eating out, I share a dessert with the whole table.

Today, I create a piece of art on my plate with my food.

Today, at each meal, I eat all the low-cal foods first.

Today, I do something that I enjoy when a food craving appears, and hopefully in ten minutes it will disappear. A glass of water is very helpful.

Today, I do not eat candies or chocolate. My cravings may begin to disappear, especially if I do this again the next day and the next!

Today, I increase the "density" of my foods, eating food containing more water and fiber.

Today, at each meal I set the table with beauty: silver, crystal, pretty linens, flowers, and candles.

Today, I put several different small portions of foods, rather than one large portion of a single food, on my plate. It is so much more interesting.

Today, I use the foods that are naturally in season as much as possible. I anticipate the annual changes and I use a variety of colour and texture on my plate.

Today, I shop at local markets where all the food products are grown or raised within one hundred miles of my home. This helps reduce the carbon footprint on our Earth.

Today, I walk up several flights of stairs. I avoid elevators and escalators.

Today, I drink two more glasses of water.

Mindful Eating Ideas

Like the Mokens, an Austronesian ethnic group, I am mindful not to say or use the word "want".

When I feel my energy is low, I take notice of what I am doing and then what I do about it – that is, what action I take. I observe how this relates to food and my eating habits and patterns.

I focus my attention on doing one thing at a time, I no longer multi-task.

I eat no junk food snacks or fast food in order to minimize my consumption of fast food.

I remember I am a human being and not a cow or a sheep, so I will not graze!

I avoid "see-food eating"(not sea food)!   In other words, "eating all the food I see"!

I pay attention to see if I use eating to reduce stress.

I am aware that my eyes (my perceptions) don't sometimes see the "real" size of servings.

I don't step on the weigh-scale. Rather, I believe the tightness of my clothes.

I am become aware of all the comfort foods I consume.

I say out loud, "I am not hungry; however, I am going to eat it anyway." I examine this statement. It allows me to recognize and acknowledge my stomach's true needs.

I avoid putting lots of small dishes with a variety of foods out on the table: doing this will only encourage me to overeat.

I realize I have control over what I put in my mouth.

I am conscious of when I use the words "should" or "should not."

I am mindful to stop eating and not continue to eat after I feel full.

When shopping, I am mindful of what is healthy or not healthy in my shopping basket.

I realize that I can try to eat all my meals fully in the present moment, just one meal at a time.

I use my creative energies to create the kind of food I love to eat.

I am aware that eating too much sugar could promote diabetes.

I am aware that extra weight can cause back or knee pain.

I am aware that extra weight can cause breathing problems.

I am aware that I need to drink, drink, drink lots of water, especially before a meal.

I am aware my stomach is only fist-sized! I realize I can use my hand size for a portion size.

I think of trimming calories as one side of a coin and burning calories as the reverse side – I need both for balance.

I am mindful of not only what I eat, but also the portion size I eat, I will keep eating my style of food, but much less of it.

I think about fuelling my body, not feeding my body. I do this with healthy foods.

When I have failed with one meal or skipped exercising, I don't get into the negative "I'll give it all up" mindset. I am a human being, not a robot! I know I can always begin anew in this moment.

I mindfully tell unsupportive family and friends how I feel when they sabotage me with negative talk or encourage me to eat. I use "I" statements, not "you" statements, to tell them how I feel.

I treat myself early in the day to some exercise, when maybe later I won't find the time to do it or I feel too tired.

I make non-judgmental choices about my eating and myself.

I am mindful of my pre-eating and post-eating feelings.

I am observant and accepting of most of my thoughts.

I focus my thoughts on "The Now", whenever they wander from the present moment into the past or future.

I am grateful for my marvelously alive body.

"I eat until I am eight-tenths full." (An old Chinese saying.)

With each meal, my largest portions are always vegetables; my smallest portion is always protein.

I am aware that increasing my mindfulness of eating can help me make changes with other habit energies.

I make my Mondays "Mindful Mondays" and go on a liquid or all fruit fast for the day. I feel cleansed and the discipline is great.

I shop only when I need food. Fresh food always tastes better.

I focus on all my five senses to tell me what is happening around me and how I am responding.

I regularly try new herbs and spices in my recipes.

I realize that visual variety in food presentation entertains my mind. As well as keeping my stomach content, it keeps my mind interested and alert.

"Words to live by are just words, unless you actually live by them"
-ERIC HARVEY AND STEVE VENTURA

I look at changing some of my cultural learned attitudes toward food.

With each meal I do not bore myself with only one food group.

I eat with my stomach, not with my head.

I know less can actually be more!

Hindrances and Supportive Practices

Hindrances prevent you from living
a peaceful and happy life.

Hindrances to practicing A Mindful Diet are your mind-roadblocks. They could be not choosing to write down any exercises from this book to follow on a daily basis. Or a Hindrance could be allowing you to get upset that you are not acting upon your chosen habit energy changes, giving up and so falling off your A Mindful Diet program!

Thich Nhat Hanh teaches, "Forgetfulness is our greatest enemy". I too believe our greatest hindrance is our own forgetfulness. When you forget to be mindful or aware, you can so easily go back to our old habit energies, ones that have not worked for you in the past. Only by changing these old habit energies and ideas, and replacing them with new ones, will you benefit from any changes in your eating habits.

Shame could be another Hindrance, either about not being strong enough to change one's eating habit energies in that moment, or about your present mindlessness state as to your actual real physical need to eat. A Hindrance could also be embarrassment of your present body shape and size.

Only by changing these old habit energies and ideas, and replacing them with new ones, will you benefit from any changes in your eating awareness. If you can practice **The Five Contemplations** plus two exercises, for four weeks, you could be well on your way to a lifetime of new eating awareness.

To assist you from falling into this trap of forgetfulness or non-change you need some Supportive Practices.

Hindrances
and Supportive
Practices

Supportive Practices assist you in
living a peaceful and happy life.

The most supportive practice for following A Mindful Diet is **The Five Contemplations**. To recite the Five Contemplations before eating and to be mindful of what you are expressing with these words. A second very supportive practice is to repeat **The Five Mindfulness Trainings** daily and to understand fully what they mean in your way of living.

Another Supportive Practice is to be aware that mindfulness of your body and feelings is crucial to knowing when and what to eat, and when and what not to eat. To be aware that eating is not necessarily just a physical need, but to become aware of the times you are eating only because of your emotional needs. You need to be aware of these different feelings in your own body and this can only done by practicing awareness of your own body and feelings.

A very Supportive Practice is to have a like-minded friend to call upon at any time, or to form A Mindful Diet Group to discuss your actions, feelings and fears and successes.

The simplest Supportive Practice is just to STOP what you are thinking or doing, breathe three times, and say to myself, "In this moment I can begin anew and change my habit energy".

And as with any other practice in life, it is all about practice, practice and more practice!

Community by Thich Nhat Hahn

The other miracle is the community in which everyone is practicing in the same way. The woman sitting next to me is also practicing mindfulness while eating her breakfast. How wonderful! She is touching the food with mindfulness. She is enjoying every morsel of her breakfast, like me. We are brother and sister on the path of practice. From time to time we look at each other and smile. It is the smile of awareness. It proves that we are happy, that we are alive. It is not a diplomatic smile. It is a smile born from the ground of enlightenment, of happiness.

That smile has the power to heal. It can heal you and your friend. When you smile like that, the woman next to you will smile back. Before that, maybe her smile was not completely ripe. It was ninety percent ripe. If you offer her your mindful smile, you will give her the energy to smile one hundred percent.

When she is smiling, healing begins to take place in her. You are very important for her transformation and healing. That is why the presence of brothers and sisters in the practice is so important. This is also why we don't talk during breakfast. If we talk about the weather or the political situation in the world, we can never say enough.

We need the silence to enjoy our own presence and the presence of our brothers and sisters. This kind of silence is very alive, powerful, nourishing, and transforming. It is not oppressive or sad. Together we can create this kind of noble silence. It is sometimes described as "thundering silence" because it is so powerful.

Silent Eating

The Venerable Thich Nhat Hanh is a Zen Master who has been teaching the art of mindfulness throughout the world for over forty years. He resides at Plum Village Retreat Centre in France and has written numerous books on the practice of mindfulness. Dr. Martin Luther King, for the Nobel Peace Prize in 1966, nominated Thich Nhat Hanh.

The following has been taken from a handout given at Plum Village in France. It has been edited for clarity and grammar, but is otherwise the same as the original.

"The purpose of eating a meal in silence is to help you appreciate the food, the company of others, and the practice of mindfulness. At first it may seem awkward or embarrassing; however, it will eventually become a delight. It benefits not only your digestion; your entire being – body and mind – will benefit as the silence brings you a sense of peace, calm, and awareness.

"All your life, food has been provided for you either by your parents, your friends, your teachers, your spouse, or through your job, your work with an employer. Directly and indirectly, the universe has provided you with your daily nourishment. Many others have been involved with this process. Give silent gratitude and pay fuller attention to the food you are now eating, it will help you to become fully awake to all that you are and do.

"Every piece of food contains the sun and the life of our Earth. You share this life with all beings everywhere. Before beginning your silent eating, give thanks for your food by saying **The Five Contemplations**.   Mindful eating will then become a daily mindful practice to you."

After eating I can say to myself:
"My plate is empty, and my hunger is satisfied.
I will try to live for the benefit of all beings."

When I am washing the dishes I can say to myself:
"Washing the dishes is like bathing a baby.
The profane is the sacred."
Thich Nhat Hanh

The Five
Mindfulness
Trainings

"The next message you need is always right where you are."
-Ram Dass

Beginnings are always so intoxicating. Turning over a new leaf, writing on a clean slate – just like New Year's resolutions. You can be hopeful and view A Mindful Diet as the start of something big. However, this book emphasizes small steps, perhaps only a single small change forever.

There are many ideas, and it is your choice to follow the step or steps that seem just right for you. As it says in the Tao, "A journey of a thousand miles starts with a single step." Forget about the miles and just concentrate on one step at a time. One moment at a time, after all, is what mindfulness is all about – moment-by-moment awareness and enjoyment. This is what Eckhart Tolle means when he tells us about the "is-ness of now" in his marvelous, best-selling book, "The Power of Now".

The Five Mindfulness Trainings, written and developed by Thich Nhat Hanh, are called trainings because they are exactly that – trainings **not** rules. They were created only to assist you in living mindfully. They have nothing to do with religion; in fact, it is felt that practicing your own religious beliefs will help you in being more mindful and thus better understand those beliefs.

The Five
Mindfulness
Training

Each of The Five Mindfulness Trainings begins with the words, **"Aware of the suffering caused by..."** This is one of the most important aspects of these trainings, for until you are aware that you are suffering, you will never do anything to change your suffering.

So to assist you with your A Mindful Diet journey, try to practice just one of The Five Mindfulness Trainings every day. If you do, you will discover they can be the fundamental keys to your success in attaining mindfulness. In fact, when you find you are practicing just one of the trainings, you will discover that you are actually practicing all five!

THE FIRST MINDFULNESS TRAINING

Reverence for all life

Positive traits developed – kindness and compassion

"Aware of the suffering caused by the destruction of life, I am committed to cultivating compassion and learning ways to protect the lives of people, animals, plants, and minerals. I am determined not to kill, not to let others kill, and not to support any act of killing in the world, in my thinking, and in my way of life."

The Second Mindfulness Training

Do not take that which does not belong to you

Positive trait developed – generosity

"Aware of the suffering caused by exploitation, social injustice, stealing, and oppression, I am committed to cultivating loving kindness and learning ways to work for the well-being of people, animals, plants, and minerals. I will practice generosity by sharing my time, energy, and material resources with those who are in real need. I am determined not to steal and not to possess anything that should belong to others. I will respect the property of others, and I will prevent others from profiting from human suffering or the suffering of other species on Earth."

The Third Mindfulness Training

Conscious sexuality

Positive trait developed – joyous satisfaction in yourself and your partner

"Aware of the suffering caused by sexual misconduct, I am committed to cultivating responsibility and learning ways to protect the safety and integrity of individuals, couples, families, and society. I am determined not to engage in sexual relations without love and a long-term commitment. To preserve the happiness of others and myself, I am determined to respect my own commitments and the commitments of others. I will do everything in my power to protect children from sexual abuse and to prevent couples and families from being broken apart by sexual misconduct."

THE FOURTH MINDFULNESS TRAINING

Skilful speech and mindful listening

Positive trait developed – seeking loving truth

"Aware of the suffering caused by unmindful speech and the inability to listen to others, I am committed to cultivating loving speech and deep listening in order to bring joy and happiness to others and relieve them of their suffering. Knowing that words can create happiness or suffering, I am determined to learn to speak truthfully, with words that inspire self-confidence, joy, and hope. I will not spread news that I do not know to be certain and will not criticize or condemn things of which I am not sure. I will refrain from uttering words that can cause division or discord, or that can cause the family or the community to break. I am determined to make all efforts to reconcile and resolve all conflicts."

THE FIFTH MINDFULNESS TRAINING

Mindful consumption

Positive traits developed – mindfulness, contentment, and awareness

"Aware of the suffering caused by unmindful consumption, I am committed to cultivating good health, both physical and mental, for myself, my family, and my society by practicing mindful eating, drinking, and consuming. I will ingest only items that preserve peace, well-being, and joy in my body, in my consciousness, and in the collective consciousness of my family and society. I am determined not to use alcohol or any other intoxicant. I will not ingest foods or consume other items that contain toxins, such as certain music, TV programs, magazines, books, films, and conversations. I am aware that to damage my body or my consciousness with these poisons is to betray my ancestors, my parents, my society, and future generations. I will work to transform violence, fear, anger, and confusion in myself and in society by practicing a diet for myself and for society. I understand that a proper diet is crucial for self-transformation and for the transformation of society."

"The truth knocks on the door and you say, 'Go away; I am looking for the truth.' And so it goes away."

-ROBERT M. PIRSIG

Five Skillful Habits
An Ethics-based
Mindfulness Intervention

The following is from a paper presented by Lynette Monteiro, PhD. and R. Frank Musten, PhD. at the 4th International Conference on Spirituality and Mental Health, April 24 2009, Ottawa, Canada.

"The Five Mindfulness Trainings are creative in their simplicity and secularity. There are few who would argue against practicing how to respect one's mortality, become more generous, use one's resources in a sustainable way, speak with compassion, and be physically and emotionally ecologically-minded in all activities. The appeal of The Five Mindfulness Trainings is in their encouragement to engage in the process of becoming aware of intended and unintended consequences before engaging in an action or thought. That is, they are not about right or wrong actions but about cultivating oneself so that there is a seamless continuity of awareness and a progression in skillfulness.

The adaptation of The Five Mindfulness Trainings to reflect more strongly the behavioral aspects of practice have been a useful and beneficial component of the overall Mindfulness-Based interventions offered at the Ottawa Mindfulness Clinic. As the Five Skillful Habits, they have provided a formal guide to the development of mindfulness and taken some of the mystery out of the details of how to practice. By providing a clear focus in each week of an ethically derived way to establish mindfulness, the skills accrue in strength and are more easily re-directed towards healthy choices."

The FIVE Skillful Habits to develop	BODY	EMOTIONS	SENSATIONS	THOUGHTS
Skillful reverence for all life. (Kindness and Compassion)				
Skillful use of resources. (Generosity)				
Skillful attention to boundaries. (Joy in Relationships)				
Skillful attention to speech and listening. (Seeking truth)				
Skillful consumption. (Mindfulness, contentment, awareness)				

Table 1: Five Skillful Habits (The Five Mindfulness Trainings) to develop.

The FIVE Skillful Habits to develop	BODY	EMOTIONS	SENSATIONS	THOUGHTS
Skillful Reverence for all life. (Kindness and Compassion)	While eating, paying attention to body sensations.	Attend to emotional suffering. Establish a gratitude practice, e.g. The Five Contemplations. Observe and tune into emotions.	Try not to avoid pain physical or emotional.	Attend to underlying pain when thinking violent, repetitive or unhealthy thoughts.
Skillful use of resources. (Generosity)	Exercise. Rest.	Use non-violent communication (speech/thoughts). Identify responsibility. Charitable acts.	Listening. Eating slowly.	Compassion, self-empathy, focusing.
Skillful attention to boundaries. (Joy in Relationships)	Say "no", as often as saying "yes". Take time for self and others. Take breaks. Don't over-exert self.	Express emotions in ways not harmful to self or others.	Reduce and deal with negative events/emotions.	Express gratitude. Notice good in life.

Table 2: Part 1 Examples of behaviors selected by participants to practice in the Five Skillful Habits (The Five Mindfulness Trainings).

Skillful attention to speech and listening. (Seeking truth)	Be non-judgmental about health related choices.	Express and allow emotions to exist. Express self in non-harmful ways. Choose words with care and be aware of intention behind words.	Listening with mindfulness. Be more sensitive to others' feelings. Be less critical.	Let go of negative thoughts. Welcome thoughts, but let them pass. Watch thoughts pass and refocus on the now.
Skillful consumption. (Mindfulness, contentment, awareness)	Not eat foods that are hard to digest. Choose healthy choices.	(no participants provided examples here)	Eating slowly	More relaxed. More positive. Accepting "This is me".

Table 2: Part 2 Examples of behaviors selected by participants to practice in The Five Skillful Habits (The Five Mindfulness Trainings).

Mindful Eating by Thich Nhat Hahn

Mindful eating is very pleasant. We sit beautifully. We are aware of the people that are sitting around us. We are aware of the food on our plates. This is a deep practice. Each morsel of food is an ambassador from the cosmos. When we pick up a piece of a vegetable, we look at it for half a second. We look mindfully to really recognize the piece of food, the piece of carrot or string bean. We should know that this is a piece of carrot or a string bean. We identify it with our mindfulness: "I know this is a piece of carrot. This is a piece of string bean." It only takes a fraction of a second.

When we are mindful, we recognize what we are picking up. When we put it into our mouth, we know what we are putting into our mouth. When we chew it, we know what we are chewing. It's very simple.

Some of us, while looking at a piece of carrot, can see the whole cosmos in it, can see the sunshine in it, can see the earth in it. It has come from the whole cosmos for our nourishment.

You may like to smile to it before you put it in your mouth. When you chew it, you are aware that you are chewing a piece of carrot. Don't put anything else into your mouth, like your projects, your worries, your fear, just put the carrot in.

And when you chew, chew only the carrot, not your projects or your ideas. You are capable of living in the present moment, in the here and the now. It is simple, but you need some training to just enjoy the piece of carrot. This is a miracle.

I often teach "orange meditation" to my students. We spend time sitting together, each enjoying an orange. Placing the orange on the palm of our hand, we look at it while breathing in and out, so that the orange becomes a reality. If we are not here, totally present, the orange isn't here either.

There are some people who eat an orange, but don't really eat it. They eat their sorrow, fear, anger, past, and future. They are not really present, with body and mind united.

When you practice mindful breathing, you become truly present. If you are here, life is also here. The orange is the ambassador of life. When you look at the orange, you discover that it is nothing less than fruit growing, turning yellow, becoming orange, the acid becoming sugar. The orange tree took time to create this masterpiece.

When you are truly here, contemplating the orange, breathing and smiling, the orange becomes a miracle. It is enough to bring you a lot of happiness. You peel the orange, smell it, take a section, and put it in your mouth mindfully, fully aware of the juice on your tongue. This is eating an orange in mindfulness. It makes the miracle of life possible. It makes joy possible.

Acknowledgments

I thank my most beloved teacher "Thay", Zen Master, The Most Venerable Thich Nhat Hanh. His wonderful mindfulness teachings and trainings have supported me now for nearly twenty years.

From the depths of my heart, I thank my dearest devoted husband and best friend John for his nearly forty-five years of total support and love. I also express my overflowing gratitude to my wonderful family, David, Mark, Timothy, Larissa, Angela, Amanda, Emily and Megan. Also for my dear sweet little mindfulness trainer and walking companion, Winston Edward.

Finally, I give thanks and appreciation to all the members of my extended family and to my friends for their love, encouragement and support during my continual journey of trying to live each moment of each day mindfully.

With so much gratitude for having you all in my life,

Jeanie Seward-Magee

Bowen Island, B.C., Canada
2009